Surf's Up, Bulldogs!

An Adult Coloring Book of English Bulldogs Riding the Waves

Welcome to "Surf's Up, Bulldogs!" An Adult Coloring Book of English Bulldogs Riding the Waves. In this coloring book, you will find a collection of lively illustrations featuring our favorite four-legged friends, surfing and having fun in the sun.

This book is a tribute to the free spirit of these lovable animals and a celebration of the carefree beach lifestyle. As you dive into the pages of this book, you will find yourself transported to a world where the sun is always shining, the waves are always perfect, and the bulldogs are always ready for adventure.

Each illustration is carefully crafted to capture the charm and personality of these furry surfers. The intricate details and varied complexity of these designs make them a joy to color, whether you're a beginner or an experienced artist.

But this book is more than just a coloring book. It's an invitation to escape the daily grind, relax, and let your creativity soar. It's a reminder to embrace the joy of living in the moment and to never take life too seriously.

So grab your favorite coloring tools, find a comfortable spot, and get ready to ride the waves of creativity. Whether you're looking for a fun way to unwind or seeking inspiration for your next adventure, "Surf's Up, Bulldogs!" is the perfect companion.

Happy Coloring!